This edition published in 1995
by SMITHMARK Publishers Inc.
16 East 32nd Street
New York
NY 10016
USA

SMITHMARK books are available for bulk
purchase for sales and promotion and premium
use. For details write or call the
manager of special sales,
SMITHMARK Publishers Inc.
16 East 32nd Street
New York
NY 10016
(212) 532–6600

© Anness Publishing Limited 1995

Produced by
Anness Publishing Limited
Boundary Row Studios
1 Boundary Row
London SE1 8HP

ISBN 0 8317 1148 5

Editorial Director Joanna Lorenz
Editorial Consultant Jackie Fortey
Project Editor Belinda Wilkinson

Printed and bound in China

A Storyteller Book

Snow White

by Jakob and Wilhelm Grimm

Retold by Lesley Young

Illustrated by Brian Robertson

SMITHMARK

In the middle of winter, when the snow was falling as thickly as feathers, a queen sat at her window, sewing. She pushed open the black ebony window frame to see how deep the snow was. As she leaned forward, her needle pricked her finger and three drops of blood fell on to the snow on the window sill. It looked so pretty that the queen said, "I wish I could have a child with skin as white as snow, lips as red as blood and hair as black as ebony."

Soon afterwards, the queen had a daughter, and when she looked at her she saw that her wish had come true; the child had skin as white as snow, lips as red as blood and hair as black as ebony. "You will be called Snow White," said the queen, smiling down at the baby, and then she sighed and died.

After a while, the king married again. The new queen was very vain and couldn't bear to think that anyone was more beautiful than she was. She had brought with her a magic mirror which hung in her room in the palace, and she would often stand in front of it and ask,

"Mirror, mirror, hanging there,
Who in all the land's most fair?"
And the mirror would answer,
"O Queen, I always tell what's true,
The fairest in the land is you."

Meanwhile Snow White was growing up, and becoming more beautiful every year. One day, when the queen asked the mirror who was the fairest in the land, the mirror replied,

"Your beauty shines, as ever, bright,
But the fairest one is now Snow White."

When she heard this, the queen turned pale with rage. Every time she saw Snow White, she felt ill and trembled all over.

At last she could stand it no longer. She sent for the palace huntsman and told him, "Take Snow White into the deepest part of the forest and kill her."

When she saw the look of horror on his face, the wicked queen added, "And bring me back her heart, so that I know she is dead." The huntsman and Snow White walked until they came to the very heart of the forest, where the sun struggled to get through the trees. Snow White ran ahead, gathering a bunch of flowers, but she dropped them and screamed when the huntsman drew his knife and pointed it at her.

"It's no use," he cried, "The Queen wants me to kill you, but I can't do it. Run Snow White – run for your life."

Then the huntsman killed a young deer, cut out its heart and took it back to the wicked queen, whose eyes lit up when she saw it. At last I am rid of her," she said.

Deep in the forest, Snow White was running as fast as she could, with tears streaming down her face, so that she couldn't see where she was going. She bumped into trees and thorn bushes pulled at her clothes. Wild animals watched her rushing past, but none of them harmed her.

At last, as it began to grow dark, Snow White came upon a clearing in the forest with a cottage in it. She looked in through the window, but she could see no one.

"Perhaps I can rest here," she said to herself, pushing open the door and stepping inside.

There was a table spread with a thick white cloth. On it were seven small plates, with bread and cheese on them, seven knives and forks and seven mugs full to the brim with apple juice.

Against the wall were seven little beds with thick cotton quilts. "What tidy children!" said Snow White, "but where do the parents sleep?"

She was so hungry that she took a little bit of bread and cheese from each plate, washed down with a few drops of juice, and then she curled up on one of the small beds and fell asleep.

It was completely dark when seven lanterns bobbed up the path to the cottage. They were carried by seven dwarfs – little men who earned their living by digging in the mountains for gold. "What's this?" exclaimed the first dwarf when he had pushed open the door. "Our chairs are pulled out – and look, there's mud on the floor." "Look – crumbs!" said the second, pointing at the table. "Someone's been nibbling at our supper."

"Someone's been in here," said a third dwarf, scratching his long beard.

"What do you mean, 'been'?" whispered another of the little men, bending over one of the beds, "Who's this?" All the dwarfs clustered round, and one held a candle up to look at Snow White.

"It's a child – and look how beautiful she is!"

"Sh! Let her sleep," said the dwarf whose bed it was. "I will curl up on the hearth rug, and then if she wakes in the night and needs anything, I will be ready."

The dwarfs ate their supper as quietly as they could. Every night they had bread and cheese, because they had never learned to cook. They used to dream of stew and dumplings and strawberry shortcake.

Every now and then the dwarfs stopped eating and looked over at Snow White, sleeping peacefully, her face lit by the flickering candle.

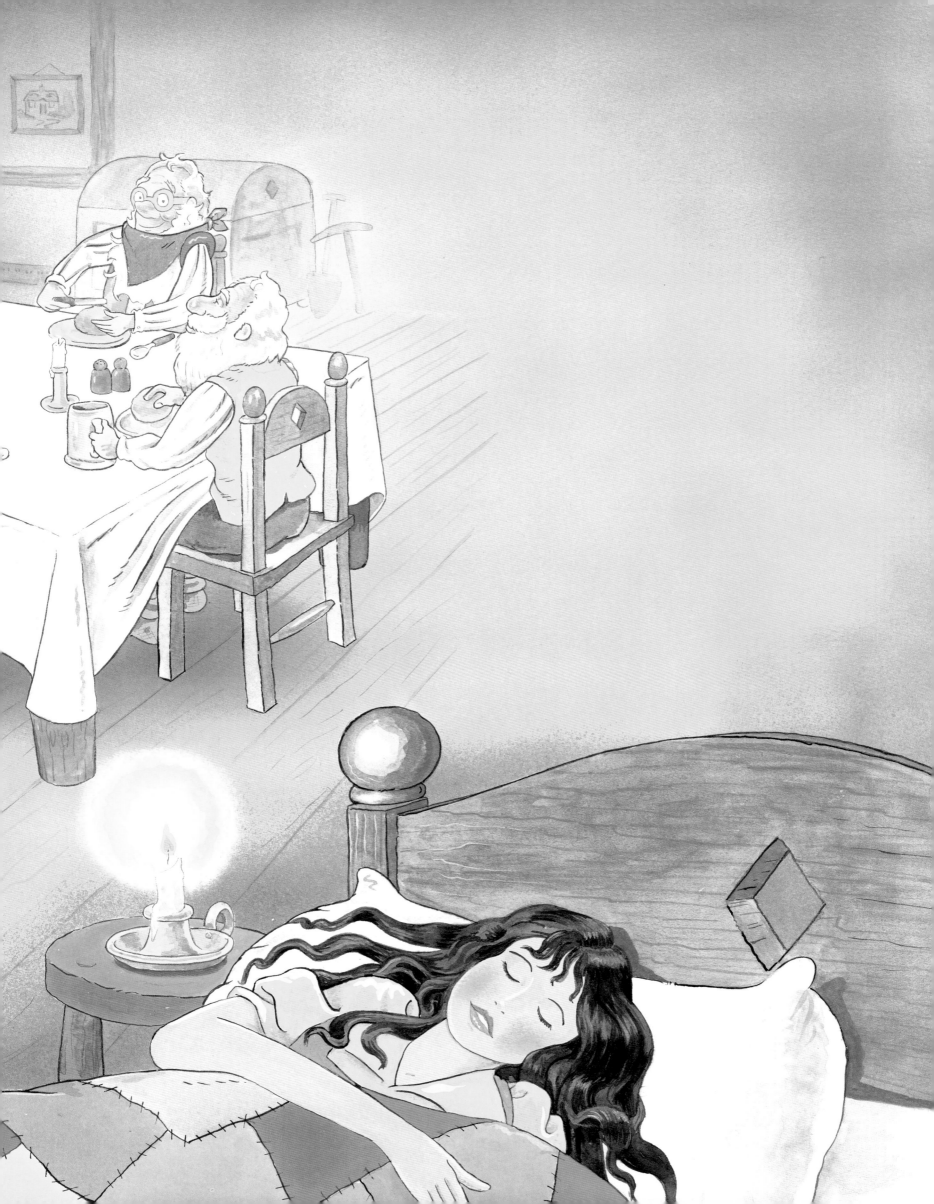

After clearing away the supper things, the dwarfs washed, changed into their night shirts and climbed into bed.

"In the morning she will tell us her story and how she came to be here," they said.

Then they snuggled down and went to sleep, as excited as if it were Christmas Eve.

In the morning, Snow White sat up in bed and yawned, stretching her arms in the air. Then she rubbed her eyes. At the end of her bed were seven little men, all watching her.

"Oh!" she cried, "Where am I? And who are you?"

"Don't be frightened. We were wondering who you were," said one of the dwarfs, rushing off to fetch a tray with bread and butter and a mug of milk.

Between sips and bites, Snow White told them about her stepmother, the wicked queen.

"She wanted the huntsman to kill me," she said, and a tear dropped onto the tray, "but he wouldn't. I ran, and ran, and now here I am."

"And here you'll stay," said the dwarfs. "You can keep house for us while we go to work."

"Can I?" asked Snow White, cheering up. "Do you by any chance," she added, looking round at them all shyly, "like apple pie?"

The dwarfs began dancing with one another, shouting, "Hurrah! Apple pie for supper."

"Now, remember," they told Snow White when they left for work, their picks over their shoulders, "don't open the door to anyone. The queen will soon find out where you are and will come looking for you."

"I promise," said Snow White. "Now off you go. There will be a hot supper waiting for you tonight."

At the palace, the queen climbed the stairs to her room. Snow White was dead. The wicked queen went and stood in front of the magic mirror and asked,

"Mirror, mirror, hanging there,
Who in all the land's most fair?"

But the mirror answered,

"With seven dwarfs in a cottage small,
Lives Snow White – fairest of them all."

When she heard this, the queen knew that the huntsman had tricked her.

"He may have saved Snow White's life," she snarled, rushing from the room, "but not for long."

Down in the palace basement, the queen stirred some poison in a bowl until it bubbled and fizzed. She soaked a comb in the poison and put it in a basket together with some handkerchiefs and soap. Then she opened a trunk of old clothes and dressed herself in rags with a black cape over the top. She pulled on a gray, straggly wig and covered her face with thick make-up and a layer of white powder, until she looked like a poor, old woman.

Finally she put the basket over her arm, took a walking stick and hobbled out of the palace gates.

Snow White was busy making pie when she heard a voice calling outside: "Pretty goods for sale!"

'The dwarfs warned me not to let anyone in,' thought Snow White, looking out of the window, 'but this is only a poor old woman. What harm could she do me?' So she wiped her floury hands on her apron and opened the door to let her in.

"Is there anything here that catches your eye, my pretty one?" cackled the old woman.

The poison made the comb glisten with all the shades of the rainbow, and Snow White longed to pick it up.

"This comb would look lovely against your black hair," said the old woman. "Shall I put it on for you?"

"Yes, please," said Snow White. The wicked queen stuck the comb into Snow White's hair. At once Snow White fell down senseless at her feet.

"Ha!" laughed the queen. "Who's the fairest now?" and she threw down her walking stick and hurried back to the palace.

When their work was finished for the day, the seven dwarfs
hurried back to their cottage. "I don't smell any pie," said one as
they reached the clearing. "And what's this?" asked another as
he picked up the walking stick the queen had dropped.

They rushed inside and found Snow White lying on the floor.

"She's dead," cried one, but when they picked her up to carry
her to a bed, their lanterns shone on the poisoned comb.

"Look at that – quick, pull it out," said a dwarf.

So they pulled out the comb and soon Snow White was
sitting up and telling them what had happened.

"That 'poor old woman' was the wicked queen," they said.
"She is clever and she will disguise herself in lots of ways.
Remember, you must not open the door to anyone."

At the palace, the queen threw off her rags, wiped her face clean, and went to her magic mirror.

"*Mirror, mirror, hanging there,*
Who in all the land's most fair?"

She just couldn't believe it when the mirror still gave the same answer as before:

"*With seven dwarfs in a cottage small,*
Lives Snow White – fairest of them all."

"Just wait," said the queen, "I can mix up a stronger poison."

Weeks passed and the dwarfs grew to love Snow White. They rushed home from their work in the mines, and as they reached the clearing they would sniff the smell of cooking in the air and shout out: "Chicken stew!" or "Apple dumplings!"

There was always a wonderful hot supper waiting for them, and flowers in a vase on the table. The shelves in the pantry were weighed down with cakes and pies.

"We never knew we were lonely until you arrived," they told Snow White. "Just think – seven of us and we were all lonely, but never again."

The queen had other plans. In the palace basement she was brewing up an even stronger poison. When it was ready, she took a green apple and dipped half of it in the poison. The half that was dipped came out a bright rosy red, so shiny that whoever saw it would long to sink their teeth into it.

This time, the queen disguised herself as a tramp, with a brown, weatherbeaten face and thick boots, and set off into the forest with a basket of apples.

"Ripe, rosy apples!" she called as she marched into the clearing where the dwarfs' cottage stood.

Snow White stuck her head out of the window. "I can't open this door to anyone. The dwarfs made me promise."

"Quite right too!" said the wicked queen. "What a sensible girl – here, let me give you an apple."

"No," said Snow White politely, "I promised not to take any presents."

"I suppose you're worried about poison," laughed the queen, "Look – I'll eat half of this apple, just to show you how safe it is."

She took a knife and cut the apple in half and took a big bite of the green side.

"There – I've saved the best half for you, my dear," she said, holding it out.

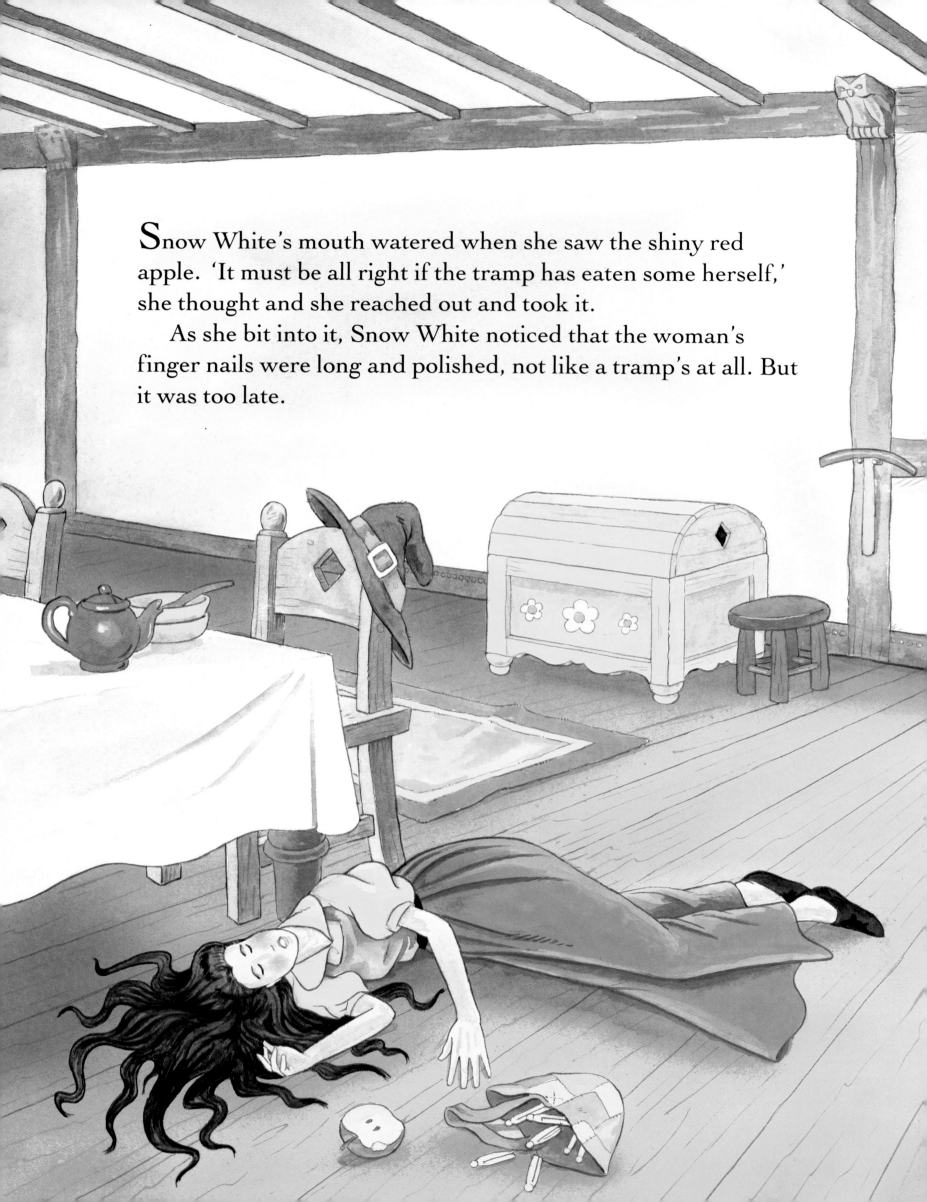

Snow White's mouth watered when she saw the shiny red apple. 'It must be all right if the tramp has eaten some herself,' she thought and she reached out and took it.

As she bit into it, Snow White noticed that the woman's finger nails were long and polished, not like a tramp's at all. But it was too late.

As soon as she bit the apple Snow White fell to the floor and lay there, dead.

The wicked queen laughed: "Let's see if the dwarfs can wake you up this time!"

When she asked the mirror
that night who was the fairest in
the land, the mirror answered,
  "O Queen, I always tell what's true,
  The fairest in the land is you."
"At last!" shouted the queen.
"At last I can have some peace!"

The dwarfs came home and found Snow White lying on the floor of their cottage, as white and as cold as snow.

They looked in her hair for a poisoned comb, but they found nothing – Snow White lay as if she were sleeping and having a lovely dream.

All the dwarfs sat round Snow White and wept. They had no heart for cleaning or cooking and the dust settled in drifts in their cottage.

After three days, they decided it was time to bury Snow White. "She looks so beautiful," sobbed one, "I can't bear to lay her in the dark earth."

"Let's make a coffin out of glass," said another," and then we can always look at her and remember how happy she made us."

So the dwarfs cut a coffin out of clear crystal and laid Snow White gently inside. They carried it to the top of a hill where the sun shone on it every morning, and one of them always sat beside it, watching over Snow White.

For many months Snow White lay in the glass coffin, looking as if she were not dead, but only sleeping.

One day, a prince was riding past and saw the sun shining on the crystal. He got off his horse and walked up the hill to see what it was. When the prince reached the top, he looked at Snow White, lying smiling inside and he thought that she was the loveliest thing he had ever seen.

"Let me have the coffin," he begged the dwarfs. "I will give you whatever you want for it."

"We would not part with it for all the gold in the mountains," said the dwarfs.

"Then let me have it as a present," said the prince. "I can't live without it, but I promise I will take great care of it always."

The dwarfs saw that the prince loved Snow White as much as they did. They finally agreed to let him take the coffin to a room in his castle. "You can visit her there whenever you want," said the prince.

"How I wish I had known her when she was alive."

The dwarfs were helping to carry the coffin down the hill, when they tripped and tumbled down the bumpy slope. The coffin jolted forward and the piece of poisoned apple fell out of Snow White's mouth. She yawned and stretched her arms, pushing up the lid of the coffin.

"Where are you taking me?" Snow White asked the dwarfs. "Is this a game?" Suddenly she saw the handsome prince, and she recognized him as the prince she had been dreaming about all the time she lay in the glass coffin.

"Oh, it's you!" she smiled, holding out her hand. He scooped her up and put her in front of him on his horse and they rode down the hill.

The dwarfs hugged one another and waved goodbye, tears of joy streaming down their faces.

"I will see you at the castle soon," called Snow White.

Snow White and the prince sent out invitations to their wedding to all of the great people in the land. However the prince himself rode to the cottage in the clearing to deliver invitations to the seven dwarfs.

"They are the most important guests," said Snow White.

The wicked queen heard that a grand wedding was planned.

"I hope the bride is not as beautiful as I am," she said, and
went to her room to ask her magic mirror once more:

"Mirror, mirror, hanging there,
Who in all the land's most fair?"

To her horror, the mirror answered,

"You know I have to say what's right.
It is the new princess – Snow White."

The queen was so filled with hate and anger that she smashed
the mirror with her fist. It shattered into a thousand pieces, and
one of them pierced her heart. She was found lying dead among
the broken glass.

Snow White and the prince were married in his castle in the mountains. The dwarfs watched proudly as she danced past in her white silk dress, and no one thought it was strange when they all threw their hats in the air and shouted, "Seven cheers for the prince and Snow White!"